I Am
Lola

By
Lori Bakewell

Print ISBN 9780578958774
Ebook ISBN 9780578958781

First edition

Published by Horse Tales
Warrenton, Virginia, USA

Contents

Preface: I Am Lola 4

Chapter 1: I Am Hopeful 6

Chapter 2: I Am Strong 14

Chapter 3: I Am Determined 22

Chapter 4: I Am Loving 30

Song Lyrics: Sing Along with Me!......... 38

Acknowledgements 48

Preface

I Am
Lola

I am a miniature horse. People call us minis and it's true that we are small, but we have big feelings! Maybe you have big feelings, too. It's okay to talk about our emotions. I will share mine first. After you read my story, maybe you will tell me what you are feeling. Everyone needs someone who will listen and understand. Minis are good at that. I bet you are, too!

WHOA!

Your emotions are the way you feel. You might be happy or sad or angry. Can you think of other emotions? It's good to talk about them!

Chapter 1

I Am
Hopeful

When I was young, my home was in a backyard. It was a nice yard, but I did not have a lot of interesting things to do. Eventually, I moved to a barn and I became a mother. My foal Mimi and I had each other but there was still something missing.

WHOA!

Do you know what a foal is? A foal is a baby horse!

Horses love purpose. We want to have things to do that make us feel helpful and needed and connected. When we do, our physical and mental health is better and we are nicer to be around. Horses like routine. We want to know what we are going to do with our humans. I didn't have a feeling of purpose or a positive routine.

WHOA!

A horse's human is a person who loves and cares for them.

One day a very nice woman saw Mimi and me, and took us to live with her mini, Johnnie. The woman took good care of us and was kind and loving. It was wonderful having a new home and a new friend, but I still wanted something more.

When Mimi was old enough to eat hay and grass, I hoped it would be time for me to find my purpose. I was thrilled when it happened! A lady who was part of a therapy horse troupe came to meet me. She thought I could join them. A therapy troupe is a group of horses and humans who visit schools, care facilities, and events to help others. The horses and the humans are specially trained. It's a lot of work.

I said goodbye to Mimi. That was sad, but I knew she had her friend Johnnie and a very good place to live. Now I began my big adventure. Would I like my new home? I hoped so! Would I make a friend? I hoped so!

My new home is perfect for me. I have a mini friend and many interesting things to do. I always hoped for the right home and the right purpose. Sometimes I felt sad and worried that it would never happen. When you feel that way, finding hope can be hard. You might feel stuck and unsure about how things will ever change. Remind yourself that hope is a choice. Even when things look bad, you can choose to have hope. That's what I did. I kept hoping.

I am Lola.
I am hopeful.

Chapter 2

I Am **Strong**

My new home is such a wonderful place. We take walks in the woods when the weather is nice. I love seeing the flowers bloom in the spring and I love hearing the leaves crunch under my hooves in the fall. Nature even smells good! I get lots of exercise and when I want shelter the **run-in stall** keeps me dry.

WHOA!

Do you know what a **run-in stall** is? A run-in stall is a shelter with an open door that horses can go into whenever they want. Run-in stalls help us stay warm in the winter, cool in the summer, and dry in the rain.

One of the best parts about moving here was meeting Possum. He showed me how to frisk and frolic and have fun being a mini. Possum knew how to kick up his heels but he was also very calm. I felt good and safe with Possum, the way you do with a best friend.

Possum was wise. He had lived a long time and he knew so many things. One day Possum got sick. I thought he would get better so we could run around the **paddock** together again, but that didn't happen. My friend Possum was very old and it was time for his life here on earth to end.

WHOA!

Do you know what a **paddock** is? A paddock is a small fenced field that horses can spend time in. Some horses even live in paddocks!

17

Saying goodbye to someone I loved was so hard. I felt sad all over and the paddock seemed very empty. Possum's human, Grace, was also sad. I understood how she felt and she understood how I felt. We shared those feelings and that helped us both.

One day someone new arrived at the farm. I thought Apple looked nice and I wanted to get to know him. We did not live together right away until everyone knew we could be friends. At first we shared a **salt lick**. I got used to Apple's scent and personality and he got used to mine. When we were ready to be friends we got to live together. Happiness filled me again!

WHOA!

Do you know what a **salt lick** is? These large blocks of salt are fun for horses to lick, and provide them with minerals that their bodies need to function at their best.

I still miss Possum and sometimes I am still sad about losing my friend. It's okay to be sad when something like that happens. Share those feelings if you can, like I did, and believe that the empty space in your life will be filled one day. Being strong doesn't mean you won't ever feel sad or scared. Being strong means you know that you will feel happy again. Believe it!

I am Lola.
I am strong.

Chapter 3

I Am
Determined

Life at Sligo Stables means I get to try new things. This makes me happy! When Possum was alive I watched him jump. Oh, he was good at it! Possum and Grace planned to go to a show where minis jump over **obstacles.** Each mini has a person running beside them and helping them with cues. Those are words or gestures that let the mini know what to do. The tricky part of a jumping show is that the rails get higher and higher.

Do you know what an **obstacle** is? In a miniature horse show, we jump over obstacles. A judge watches and evaluates our form. The jumps are made with light poles, or rails, that will fall if we bump into them so we don't get hurt.

22

Possum was an amazing jumper. He sprang into the air like a kangaroo. After Possum died, Apple was going to go to the show with Grace. But Apple did not know Grace very well yet and he was not sure what to do. Knowing your partner's voice and cues takes time. My human said I could go instead of Apple. I did not know how to be in a show but I did know Grace's voice. I was comfortable with her. I just needed to learn how to jump. It's hard to learn something new. You need to keep working on it and not give up. I was excited and also nervous. New experiences can make you feel that way!

Grace and I practiced a lot. I was not perfect while I was learning. Sometimes that frustrated me, but I kept trying until Grace felt I was ready. When we got to the show there were six other minis. They had been to competitions before and were very good jumpers. This was my first show. How would I compete with them? All I could do was try my best. I liked jumping. I knew I needed to believe in my head and in my heart that I could do it.

The first jump looked really high. I watched the other minis go right over it. When it was my turn, Grace encouraged me. She told me I was ready and that I could jump high, too. She was right!

After we all jumped, the rail went higher. Some of the minis could not **clear** that jump. I was the smallest one there and I did not have any experience in horse shows, but I kept trying. Grace believed in me. I believed in me.

WHOA!

In horse shows, horses have to try to **clear** a jump. This means that the horse must jump over the rail without knocking the rail off.

Guess what? I won second place at that show, and I won first place at my next show! We were so happy. I never knew I could do that until I tried. When you are determined to do something new, make sure your head and your heart help you. Your head learns what you need to know and keeps learning as you practice. Your heart tells you that you are amazing and capable. You can do anything! Being determined means trying again and again as your head and your heart and your friends cheer you on.

I am Lola.
I am determined.

Chapter 4

I Am
Loving

Becoming a therapy horse takes time. It all starts with handling. My human needed to know that I was comfortable being **groomed** and touched. Can you guess why that is important? Grooming keeps me clean and looking good for the visits. We go into a variety of places, including care facilities. I don't want to leave a cloud of dirt behind when we leave! When my human was first handling me she found out that I didn't enjoy having my ears touched. We worked a lot on that. I got used to how it felt. That's good, because the people we visit like to touch and pet me.

WHOA!

Grooming keeps a horse's coat healthy and lets the human look the horse over closely. Horses get their hooves picked, their coats combed and brushed, and their manes and tails brushed too!

Handling is important, but a therapy horse needs something more. A therapy horse needs to like people and interacting with them. When my human saw me rest my head in the lap of her friend without anyone telling me to, she knew I could be a therapy horse. I was learning many skills but that was not something she taught me. That was my heart.

Therapy horse evaluation is a test, so I had to work on specific skills. I needed to learn to back up in a straight line so I could leave any small space without turning around. That was easy for me. Standing still without my human right next to me was harder. We like being together! I started with a short stand on the end of the **lead rope** and worked up to the long thirty second stand. It's okay to learn a little bit at a time and build on what you know. It worked for me!

WHOA!

Sometimes horses use lead ropes. A lead rope attaches to a horse's halter. It's like a leash for a dog!

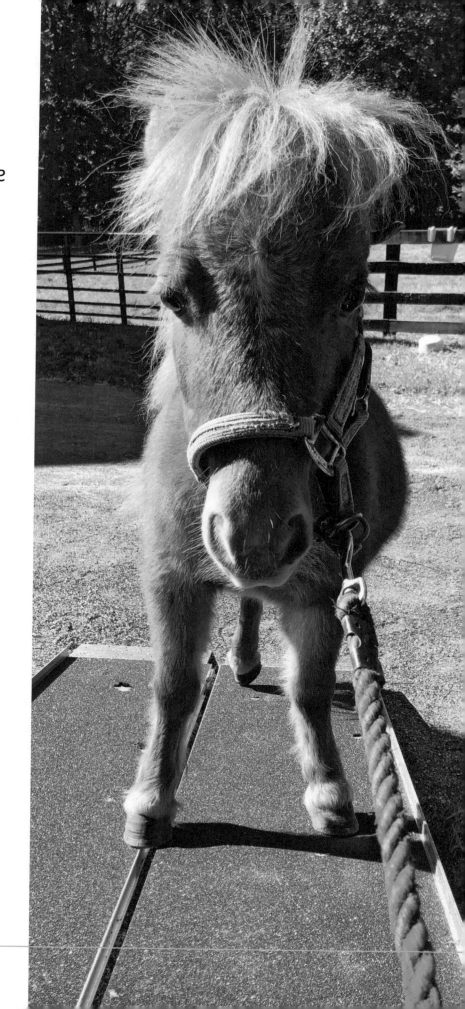

By the time we went to the evaluation I had learned so much. I knew how to get in and out of the van. My human found just the right shoes for me so I could walk inside buildings without slipping. I even learned where to go potty. That can't happen inside a building! I tried my best, but I did not pass the evaluation. Failing is hard. My human and I were sad but we were not going to let that stop us. We knew what we needed to work on and we practiced together. Failing gave us a chance to become better and stronger. The next time we were evaluated, we passed!

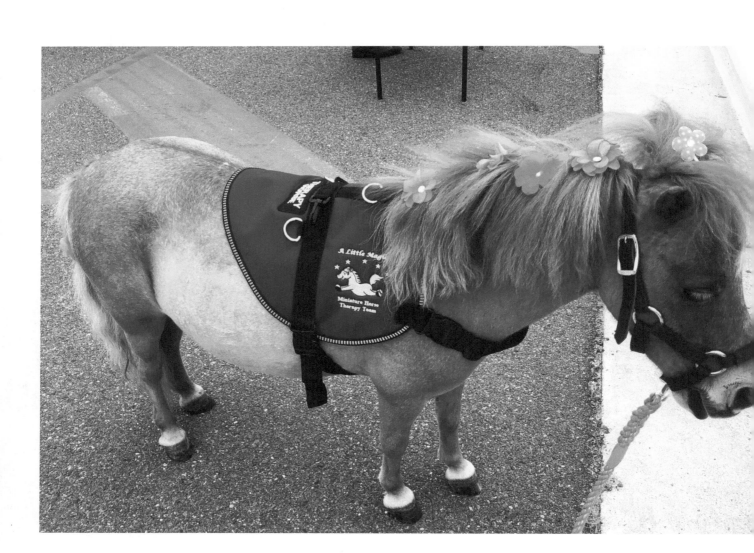

Do you remember when I wondered what my purpose would be? I found it! Becoming a therapy horse took a lot of work. It wasn't always easy but I learned something very important: when you love what you do, working hard feels good. Riding in the van and meeting people is fun. Hearing their happy voices and laughter makes me happy, too. I like doing my **tricks** and feeling gentle hands stroke my back. I love connecting with people that way.

WHOA!

Lots of therapy horses can do **tricks**. Some of my favorite tricks are shaking hands and crossing my legs. I can also kick a ball, but I don't like that one as much!

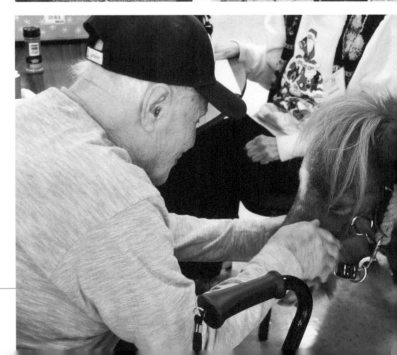

There is something else I get to do that is so wonderful. When someone doesn't have words or laughter to share, I can still be with them. Side by side, gently and quietly, we have the best part of a relationship right there with us. We have love. I like the action and the excitement of being a therapy horse but the love I share is my favorite part. When we have love, we have the possibility of anything else in the world.

I am Lola.
I am loving.

Sing Along
with Me!

Turn the page, and you will find the words to all of the songs that go along with my story. You can listen to the recordings on my website (www.horsetales.org), or any streaming service. Just search for Horse Tales or I Am Lola, and sing along with me!

I am Lola.
Sing with me!

I Am Hopeful

Song Lyrics

I'm a miniature horse with a story to tell
You see, I've had times when things didn't go well
And if you've ever struggled and had to push through
Then I'll share my story, cause it's also for you.

For most of my life, I was a backyard pet
But horses love purpose, and that need wasn't met
A kind woman saw my foal Mimi and me
Put us with her mini Johnnie, now we were three

My energy is pure, my heart is oh so true
You'll feel it when you pet me or when I look at you
So join me on my journey, I know that you will see
The places we get stuck in aren't where we're meant to be

A few months passed and weaning was a need
Mimi had to learn to eat hay and grass for feed
Soon I met a lady in a therapy horse troupe
Who thought that I could learn enough to join her group

I moved to my new home, a mini horse paradise
I have a mini friend here, and my life is quite nice
Mimi lives with Johnnie so she also has a friend
Good people take care of them—on that I depend!

If you're ever living somewhere and you know it isn't right
Don't fall into despair, and don't give up the fight
Your life can change in just an hour or two
You'll never know who you'll meet or what they can help you do

My energy is pure, my heart is oh so true
You'll feel it when you pet me or when I look at you
So join me on my journey, I know that you will see
The places we get stuck in aren't where we're meant to be

I Am Strong

Song Lyrics

Now let me tell you about the new place I live
Cause when your life is good, you have so much to give
We have logs to walk over and a run-in stall
And woods we can walk through in spring and in fall

When I arrived I met a buddy named Possum
And let me tell you, he was pretty awesome!
He'd been lots of places and took it all in stride
Sometimes his human Grace sat on him for a ride

But Possum was almost 20, which for a horse is very old
And one day he got sick, and it was his time to go
Grace stayed with him and loved him til the end
I was sad but she took care of me til I got a new friend

It didn't take long for Apple to arrive
He's bigger than me and has the kindest eye
At first we were apart but shared a salt lick
And we got to live together once we wouldn't kick!

If you ever lose a friend and you don't know what to do
Look for someone you trust to talk to
It's ok to be sad, but you can stay strong
It won't be long before a new friend comes along.
No, it won't be long before a new friend comes along.

I Am Determined

Song Lyrics

Grace and Possum were excited to go
To a charity event to jump in a show
Possum could jump like a kangaroo
While Grace ran alongside and gave him cues

Apple would soon be her partner of choice
But they had just met; he wasn't used to her voice
Sometimes he just lay down on the fence
Bringing him to jump didn't make any sense

My human said I could go in his place
Grace and I practiced jumping on pace
She said she would take me, see what we could do
I rode in the trailer with a hay net or two

Don't let anyone tell you you're not good enough
Tests can be scary and they can be tough
But regroup, stay the course, and soon you will see
You can do anything if you work hard and believe!

There were six other minis, they were amazing
I checked them out as they were grazing
They'd been to nationals and to states
Next to these champions, I felt out of place!

Then they put one jump up, the highest I'd seen
And the other horses cleared it like jumping beans
When it was my turn, I wasn't quite sure
But Grace said I could do it so I listened and soared!

Then the jump went higher; other minis dropped out
You could knock the rail down if you had any doubt
I was the smallest horse, so I had to try my best
And I came in second place; I passed the test!

Don't let anyone tell you you're not good enough
Tests can be scary and they can be tough
But regroup, stay the course, and soon you will see
You can do anything if you work hard and believe!

Grace was so proud, with a smile on her face
She told me she was thrilled with second place
Nobody knew how high I could fly
Until I cleared a jump that was bigger than I.

Regroup, stay the course, and soon you will see
You can do anything if you work hard and believe!

I Am Loving

Song Lyrics

At my new barn, I started to train
I learned whoa and back on a loose rein
To stand when I'm groomed and gently lift my hooves
When I could be sassy, and to make loving moves.

Therapy horses travel, so I had more to do
I ride in a minivan and wear teddy bear shoes
I nuzzle gently and show off all my tricks,
Learned where to go potty by listening for the clicks.

Getting what you want isn't always easy
Giving it your best isn't always breezy
But I'm not gonna say that I can't do it
I'll keep putting my heart into it

Therapy horses have to pass a test
There were lots of people there and I really tried my best
My human was sad when we failed the first time through
But we got back to work and we both learned what to do

A few months later, we passed with flying colors!
Now I'm a therapy horse, and I work with mini others.
Almost every week, I load up in my van.
We make people happy wherever we can!

Getting what you want isn't always easy
Giving it your best isn't always breezy
But I'm not gonna say that I can't do it
I'll keep putting my heart into it

My name is Lola, and I wanted to tell my tale
To show you that no matter what, you too can prevail.
Through setbacks and hardships, always stay the course.
That's what I did; now I'm a therapy horse!

Getting what you want isn't always easy
Giving it your best isn't always breezy
But I'm not gonna say that I can't do it
I'll keep putting my heart into it

I'm not gonna say that I can't do it
I'll keep putting my heart into it

Acknowledgements

The Horse Tales team is so grateful to the following, who have helped us on this journey:

Dede Shumate, for taking Lola and Mimi in, recognizing Lola's purpose as a therapy horse, and connecting her with her human.

Kristy Willwerth for providing Lola with temporary housing at Picturesque Farm.

Jordan and Grace for boarding Lola with their miniature horses, loving and caring for her every day, and supporting her therapy work in every way they can. Your horsemanship, generosity, and kindness have made all of this possible.

The women and miniature horses of A Little Magic, especially Judy Rennyson and Bettyann Senf, for providing Lola with opportunities for training visits, sharing their expertise and experience, and supporting horse and handler on their path to being a therapy horse team.

The Piedmont Equine Practice for Lola's veterinary and dental care.

Lola's "rear guards," without whom we could not have safe and comfortable visits: Alyssa Amster, Hex Amster, Mike Amster, Lori Bakewell, Pam Brunger, and all of our future recruits.

All of the people and organizations who welcomed Lola to visit, were patient with her early mistakes, and empowered her to become the therapy horse that she now is. There are far too many to name, but we are forever grateful to each and every one of you.

Maddi Mae for inspiring Lola's human to pick up a guitar after a 35-year hiatus, teaching her to write songs, workshopping them with her, and walking her through the demo process.

Alex Purdy for being Lola's English musical voice and an excellent, patient producer; and Laura Pérez (Laura Luv) and Iara Raquel for recording the vocal tracks in Spanish.

All the musicians, moms, teachers, and friends who listened to early recordings of the songs and gave us feedback and suggestions.

Mo Safren and Laura Luv for playing the I Am Lola album release party, and the local businesses who are hosting our events.

Lori Bakewell for writing Lola's story in a way that is tender, loving, humorous, and thoughtful.

Jennifer Anderson for designing Lola's book as only she can.

Sheila Glazov and Cammie Fuller for sharing their experiences on both sides of the self-publishing industry to guide us in making the best decisions.

All of the local and national media who have shared Lola's story and thus expanded her reach.

Last but not least, we owe an enormous debt of gratitude to everyone who listened to our songs, added them to a playlist, shared them with their children, believed in the messages that we wanted to share, followed us on social media, and otherwise showed support for our gentle little idea. I Am Lola, and subsequently Horse Tales, are what they are because of your support and encouragement. Thank you.

Photo Credits

Jordan Koepke Photography:
Cover photo, page 3, page 5, page 15,
page 16, bottom two photos on page 19,
page 21, page 23, page 24, page 25, page 26,
page 29, page 44

Valerie Banks Amster: Page 7, page 8,
page 9, page 11, page 25, page 17, page 18,
top photo page 19, page 27, page 32, page
33, page 34, page 39, page 40

Bettyann Senf: Page 10

Josephine Jefferson: Top photo page 35,
page 37

Hex Amster: Middle photo page 35

Rachel Pierce: Bottom photo page 35

Michael Amster: Page 13

Carl Zitzmann: Page 31, page 46

Grace Koepke: Page 42

CPSIA information can be obtained
at www.ICGtesting.com
Printed in the USA
BVHW062059290821
615496BV00001B/4